FREEDOM

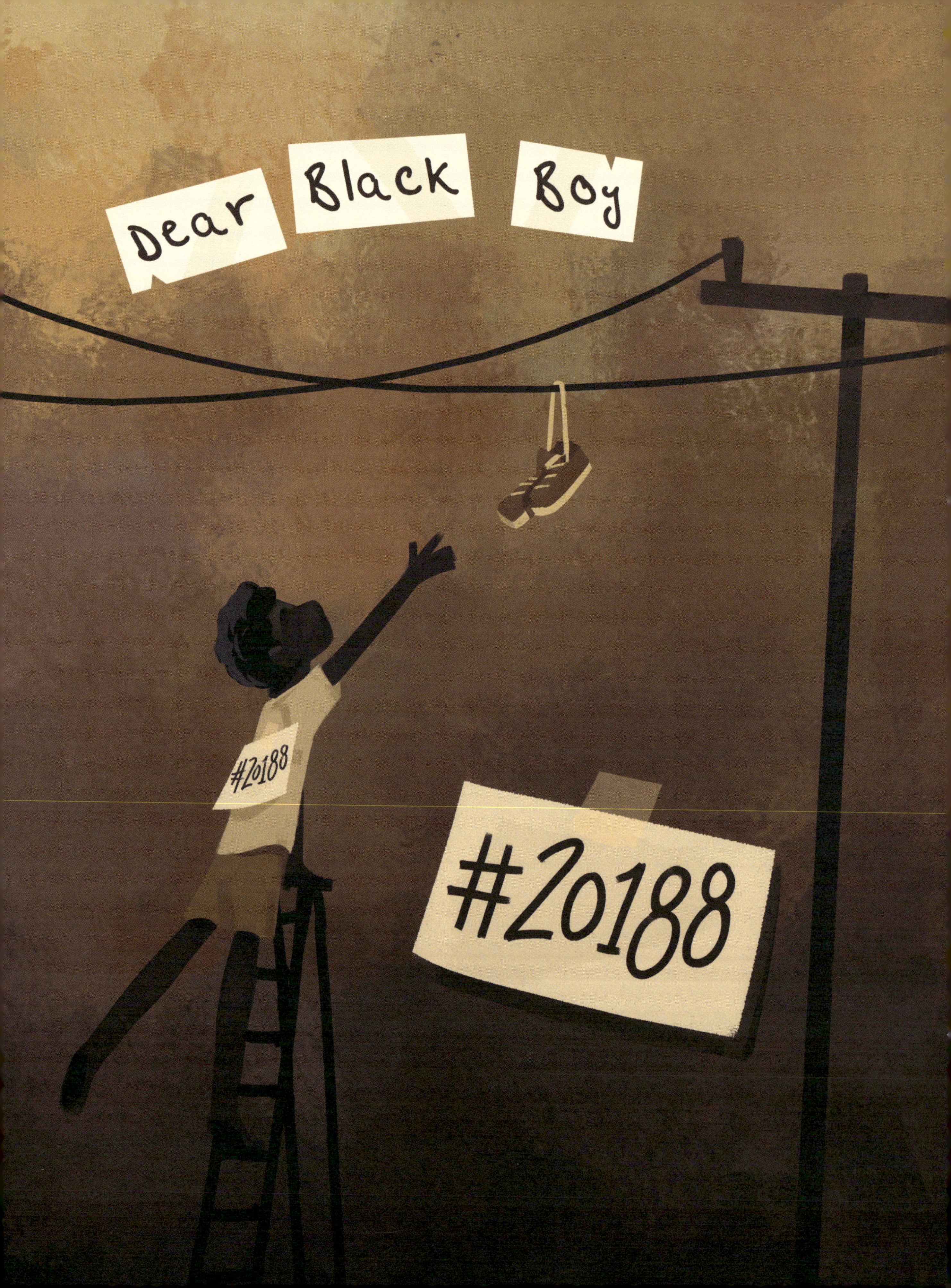
Dear Black Boy
#20188
#20188

We must lace up our shoes
to do more than
run another sprint,
dunk another ball,
catch another pass, or
swing at another pitch.

We must lace our shoes and run toward freedom—cheering on those who are training and running our same race, picking up those who get tired or distracted on their way to the finish line.

Freedom is still a giraffe and a half away. So we must run another lap, like the greats before us who ran the same race.

And we must pick up the pace.

The low-hanging fruit is what the world prefers you to reach for, but we must climb the tree.

FRESH - SQUEEZED FRUIT from the top of the tree

Climb higher and you will discover that the fruit at the top is sweeter than Kool-Aid.

The game of life is the one game
they don't think we can win...

but this must be the greatest game ever played.

Millions have marched,
millions have fought,
millions have died.

Millions continue to run for freedom.

Run,
Black Boy,
Run!

For you can change
the world
for
us
all.

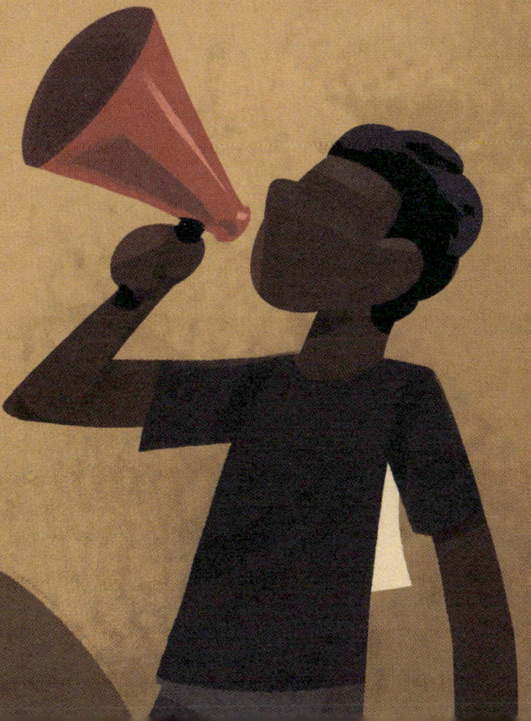

For we need you to be in shape because the journey is a long one.

Dream bigger,
Black Boy,
dream bigger!
For your dreams are valuable.
No one can take those from you.

You deserve to dream the wildest dreams and to chase those dreams the same way you chase a loose ball in the fourth quarter, a running back breaking free down the sideline, or a fly ball in the outfield.

Set goals,
Black Boy,
set goals?

Slam-dunk those goals the
same way you do an alley-oop.
For your goals in life are
worth so much more than
two points.

Shatter the glass!

Exercise,
Black Boy,
exercise!

Exercise your right to speak your mind, to pursue happiness, to seek peace and prosperity, to avoid conformity imposed by the small minds of society.

Exercise until you're drenched in sweat.

For your mind is your greatest tool.

Win,
Black Boy,
win?

For the world needs more winners who look like you.

So lace up your shoes, pick up hope, get in the game and show us what you can do.

For the game of life is
the greatest game you will
ever play.
Get out there and play
your heart out.
FREEDOM
And remember,
anything is possible!
#20188

Runners, Take Your places-

Dear Black Boy Pledge

I, _____, pledge

your name

_____

_____

_____

_____

_____

sign here

MARTELLUS BENNETT'S

IMAGINATION AGENCY STUDIOS

CREATING YOUR NEXT GREAT ADVENTURE

First published in USA by THE IMAGINATION AGENCY in 2019
ISBN: 978-0-9969820-8-5

www.theimaginationagency.com